Creative
EMBROIDERY

Creative
EMBROIDERY

Michael Lindner

HAMLYN

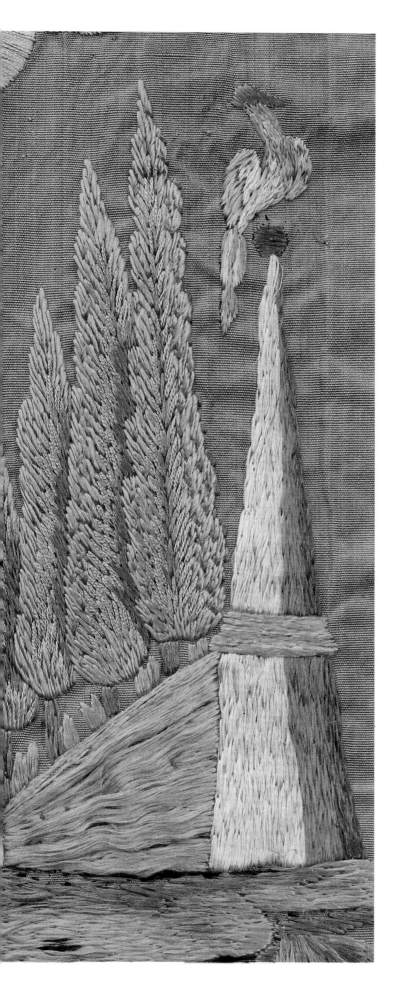

Contents

Published 1985 by
Hamlyn Publishing
Bridge House
London Road
Twickenham
Middlesex

Originally published in German under the title DAS GROSSE BUCH
VOM STICKEN
Copyright © 1984 by Xenos Verlagsgesellschaft m.b.H
Text and Design: Michael Lindner

Copyright © English text Hamlyn Publishing 1985
a division of The Hamlyn Publishing Group Limited

ISBN 0 600 50174 4

Printed in Italy

Introduction

Embroidery has for a long time had a bad image – many people felt, and some still feel, that it was a boring and tedious hobby fit only for elderly ladies with nothing better to do. But now, when the young are beginning to treasure the beautifully made clothes of their grandmothers' generation, it is fast coming back into fashion, and even those who do not actually want to do it – and it is a slow and leisurely activity not suited to everyone – can at least admire the results. The fact that this book has been written by a man tells us something about this changing attitude, in which embroidery can be regarded, not just as 'sewing' but as an art form in its own right. An interesting and little-known fact is that in the past, up until at least the seventeenth century, all professional embroiderers were men. The removal of this demanding skill from the male-dominated workshop to the ladies' parlour is a relatively recent trend and clearly a reversible one.

Another factor in the revival of interest in embroidery is probably the dissatisfaction we all feel in some measure at the modern, streamlined, factory-produced objects with which we of necessity surround ourselves. These things are not always ugly – some are indeed beautiful – and not always ill-made, but they are impersonal, and people seem to have a basic need to express their individuality and to put their personal imprint on their possessions. What better way of doing this than embroidery? By transforming 'a tablecloth' into 'my embroidered tablecloth' we fill some kind of need and make something we could not otherwise have. This could explain why embroidery originated on one of the bleaker Mediterranean islands, and why the young people of the 1960s, the 'jeans generation', went to such lengths to embellish their otherwise unremarkable clothes.

Embroidery is as old an art form as painting or sculpture – there were embroidery schools in Ancient Egypt – and like all the arts it has been used through the centuries to glorify God and to record the doings of man. We could not hope to emulate such works as the great ecclesiastical embroideries, worked in gold and silver thread, nor would we wish to, but the finest embroidered picture ever made, the Bayeux Tapestry, portraying the conquest of England by William the Conqueror, is still a source of wonder and inspiration to both designers and laymen. Wrongly called a 'tapestry', it is over 76 yards (70 metres) long and is worked in woollen threads in black and primary colours on white linen. There is no better example of embroidery as a way of 'painting with a needle'.

Creating an embroidery

These two pages show the different stages in the design and working of an embroidery from the choice of motif to the actual stitching. This embroidery is cross-stitch. The initial stages are the same for free-style embroidery, but you do not need the graph paper (stage 3).

1. To start with, choose a fairly simple motif that you won't have too much trouble drawing. The birds shown here are a good example.

2. Using a soft pencil and bold lines, transfer the pattern on to a piece of plain paper.

3. For a cross-stitch pattern place a piece of transparent graph paper over the design and fill in each cross. Alternatively, draw our motif directly on to graph paper.

4, 5. Illustration 4 shows the fine needle of a pricking machine being used to make a stencil of fine holes. Powdered charcoal or powdered chalk (depending on the colour of the fabric) is then rubbed through the holes and fixed with fixative. A simpler method is to lay a sheet of dressmaker's carbon paper between design and fabric and draw over the lines. If you do this, make sure the carbon paper is placed firmly in position and will not slip.

6. As soon as you have chosen the colours you can start the embroidery. An embroidery hoop such as the one shown here helps to keep your work clean and the fabric nice and taut so that stitching is easier, but it is not essential.

7, 8. These illustrations show two versions of the completed embroidery. A motif such as this is very versatile and can be used to decorate many different items.

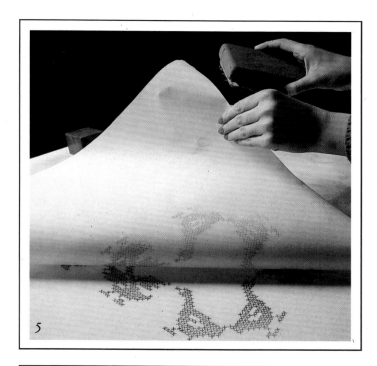

Basic guide to embroidery techniques

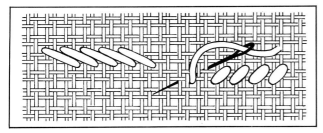

Petit point stitch

This is a canvas-work embroidery stitch, used wherever dense areas are required. Working from left to right, the thread is passed diagonally over two holes in the canvas and reinserted one hole back. The second row is worked from right to left. The stitches on the reverse are longer and more slanted than those on the correct side.

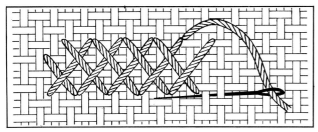

Herringbone stitch

This stitch can be used on any type of fabric. It is worked from left to right using backstitches, which lie alternately above and below the fabric. The diagram shows the needle in position for making the lower backstitch. On the right side of the fabric the diagonal threads cross one another, while on the wrong side all that is visible is two rows of small, straight stitches.

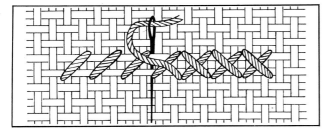

Cross-stitch (as counted-thread stitch)

Cross-stitch is best used on embroidery canvas or even-weave fabric where you can count the number of threads the cross is to go over. Work as for half-cross stitch but working a second row of diagonal stitches crossing the first. The upper half of the crosses must always lie in the same direction. The choice of how many threads of fabric you embroider over will be dictated by the type of fabric and the size of pattern. If you buy cross-stitch embroidery kits the patterns will indicate how many threads should be worked over.

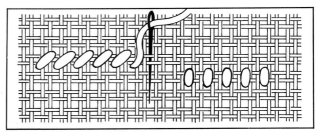

Half-cross stitch

This is also a canvas-work stitch, and looks the same as petit point stitch, but the working method is different. The thread is brought up from the back and reinserted one hole up and one hole to the right. The stitches on the back are always vertical. This is a useful stitch to use when working with thick yarn.

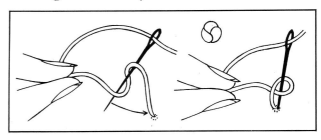

French knot

This is a free-embroidery stitch, not one used for canvas-work. It is useful for the centres of flowers and so on. Bring the needle through from the back and wrap the thread round it twice from right to left and not too loose. Hold the working thread firmly with your left hand, reinsert the needle close to where it first came through and push it back through the fabric, pulling the knot together.

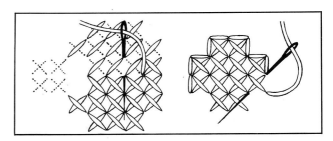

Cross-stitch (as a free-embroidery stitch)

To work cross-stitch accurately as a free stitch the crosses must first be marked on to the fabric. Any small irregularities in the drawing can be smoothed out in the embroidering. Work in exactly the same way as for cross-stitch on canvas, making sure the top threads always go in the same direction. A block of cross-stitches can be edged with backstitches for a neat effect, as shown in the diagram.

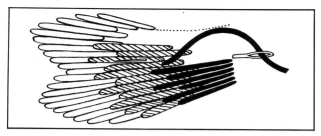

Long and short stitch

This is a variation of satin stitch using stitches of uneven lengths to give a shading effect. Different shades of the same colour are normally used to increase this effect. The first row should closely follow the outline of the shape to be filled, with the stitches being alternately long and short. The next row, usually done in a different colour, also uses long and short stitches worked in between those of the previous row, and the process is repeated till the shape is filled in.

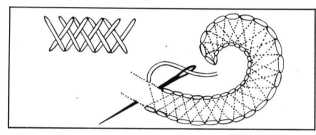

Shadow work

This is an effective way of embroidering very fine fabrics, such as net curtains, through which light will shine. It is exactly like herringbone stitch but in reverse, so that the right side of the fabric shows two rows of backstitches, while on the wrong side the diagonal threads cross over each other. When it is held up to the light, the threads at the back will show through as 'shadows'.

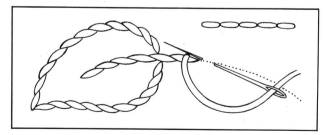

Stem stitch

As the name indicates, this stitch is suitable for stems of flowers, outlines and edgings. Working from left to right, bring the needle up from the wrong side on the line drawn on the fabric. Reinsert it about ¼ in (5 mm) along and bring it up again half-way between the entry and exit points. The thread should always come up on the left side of the previous stitch.

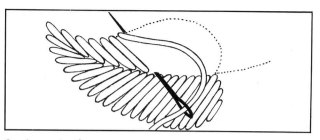

Satin stitch

This is used to fill shapes of rather smaller areas – if the stitch is too long it will pull easily. Make straight stitches as close to one another as possible until the area has been filled, and make sure you always cover the lines of any design. On canvas, satin stitch can be worked over as many threads as necessary to achieve the desired effect.

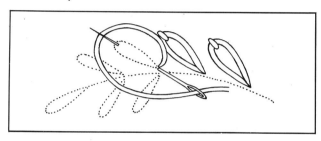

Lazy daisy stitch

This is ideal for flowers, leaves and so on where you don't want a filled-in shape, and the loops can be worked singly or in groups. Bring the thread out from below and hold it down. Reinsert the needle in the same place and bring it up a short way away (at the top of the petal). Pull the thread through gently, making a loop, and secure this with a small stitch, as shown in the diagram.

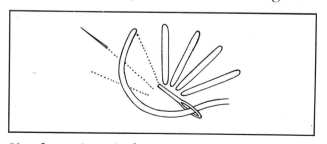

Single satin stitch

This is a variation of satin stitch in which the stitches are spaced out, and is used for any lightly embroidered flowers, leaves and so on. The stitches can be of the same size or they can vary, but they must not be too long or they will pull.

Practical hints

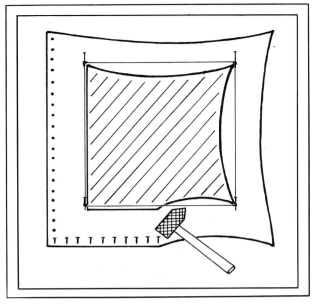

Blocking and pressing

Sometimes embroidery, particularly canvas-work, becomes very distorted during working and is hard to get back into shape. If this happens you will have to stretch it as follows. Damp the work carefully (not too much) and tack it out firmly on a board, stretching as you go and making sure that the warp and weft threads run at right angles to each other. Leave it to dry, then remove the pins and press on the wrong side using a warm iron.

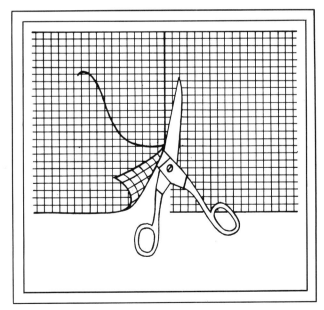

Cutting out

Make sure you always cut along the thread of a fabric or canvas, whichever type you are using. Sew up the raw edges with zigzag stitching or hem them to prevent fraying.

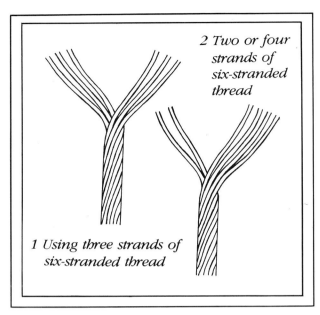

2 Two or four strands of six-stranded thread

1 Using three strands of six-stranded thread

Separating threads

The most commonly used embroidery thread is stranded cotton, which has six strands, and for delicate work it is sometimes necessary to separate the strands and work with four, three or two, or sometimes just one. In the case of bought embroidery kits the instructions will always tell you to work with either half-thickness thread (three strands) or with a certain number of strands, but sometimes you must use your judgement. The choice will depend upon the fineness of the fabric and the type of embroidery.

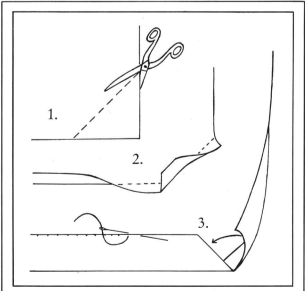

Hemming

Remember you will need approximately 1½ in (4 cm) of fabric on each side for a hem, so make sure you buy sufficient. The corners should be mitred and the hem turned inwards twice.

Drawings and transfers

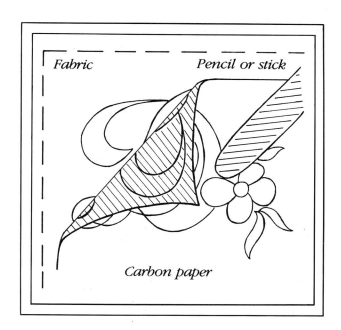

Transferring designs to fabric

In order to carry out many of the projects in this book you will need to know how to transfer designs to fabric and how to enlarge and reduce them to fit your chosen area. Neither of these processes is at all difficult. To transfer a design, make a tracing of the outlines, place a piece of dressmaker's carbon paper in a colour that will show up on the fabric beneath the tracing paper with the fabric right side up below it and pin the layers together firmly. 'Draw' over the lines on the tracing paper with a small stick, knitting needle or pencil to mark the lines on to the fabric. If you need to reverse the design, to deal with a repeat pattern, for instance, simply place the tracing paper wrong side up.

Enlarging and reducing

With the aid of a grid you can reduce or enlarge any design much more accurately than you could if you were to draw it freehand. Using a ruler and pencil draw evenly sized squares over the original design and then draw smaller or larger squares, according to whether you are reducing or enlarging, on a plain piece of paper the size you have chosen for the embroidery. Then simply transfer the design from one set of squares to the other, noting at which points the lines of the design intersect with the squares. If the design is an intricate one, work slowly to avoid mistakes.

The tools of the trade

The illustration below shows a selection of the materials used in the different branches of embroidery, canvas-work (tapestry), counted-thread work and free embroidery. There are also some artist's materials – brushes, pencils and so on. These are not essential, but you will find brushes and colours useful if you are going to design your own work or even adapt other people's designs to your own colour scheme. Felt-tipped pens in different colours make a good alternative and are inexpensive.

The opposite page describes the materials you will need and provides some information on where to obtain them.

Materials and suppliers

Fabrics

Canvas-work embroidery, sometimes called needlepoint or tapestry, is worked on even-weave stiffened canvas obtainable from needlework suppliers. There are various types: single-thread, double-thread, fine and heavy. The type you require will depend on the work you are doing, but the most commonly used is that with 10 threads to 1 inch (2·5 cm). Counted-thread embroidery (cross-stitch, etc.) is worked by counting the threads of the fabric and working each stitch over a precise number of threads. Thus even-weave fabric, in which the warp and weft have equal numbers of threads, must be used for this also. This type of fabric is usually considerably finer than the even-weave canvas described above. It is normally cotton or linen, but there are special types for special purposes, two such being hardanger fabric, specially made for this style of embroidery, and woven Aida cotton, a coarse weave which looks almost like woven ribbon. This is excellent for bold work using fairly heavy thread. Free embroidery does not need even-weave fabric, so the choice is wider. For table-cloths, napkins and so on choose a fine linen or cotton or a cotton and acrylic mixture. The synthetic 'linen-look' fabric is very good and does not crease.

Threads

For canvas-work embroidery use tapisserie wools or the matt cotton thread called soft embroidery. Knitting wools, metallic threads, silks and so on can be used for special effects, but these are recommended only for more experienced embroiderers. For counted-thread work the choice will depend on the thickness of the fabric and the size of the design. Stranded cotton, coton à broder and pearl cotton can all be used and, for bolder work on coarse-weave fabric, soft embroidery is ideal. For free embroidery stranded cotton (the number of strands depending on the fineness of the work) and pearl cotton are most usual.

Needles

For both canvas-work and counted-thread embroidery round-pointed tapestry needles are used. These are made in a range of sizes. Choose one which passes through the holes in the fabric easily without pulling the material out of shape. For free embroidery use crewel or chenille needles, the former for fine work and the latter for bolder work on heavier fabric.

Frames

It is not essential to work embroidery on a frame, but it does make it easier, particularly for canvas-work, as it keeps the fabric firm and taut. For canvas-work there are a variety of frames available: that shown opposite is just one type. Floor frames are particularly useful as they stand by themselves, leaving both hands free to work with. When buying a frame, make sure it is the right size for the work you intend to do, as a mistake could prove expensive. For counted-thread work or free embroidery hoops are used, two rings fitting one inside the other so that the fabric is stretched over the inner ring and held taut by the outer one. These hoops are made of either wood or metal, and some can be bought with a floor stand.

Suppliers

Needlework fabrics and threads as well as various needlecraft kits can be bought in some of the larger department stores, but for specialized items it is sometimes necessary to order from a specialist firm. The following firms provide a mail order service and will supply price lists or catalogues on request (enclose a stamped, addressed envelope).

The Campden Needlecraft Centre
High Street, Chipping Campden, Gloucestershire
Embroidery supplies

The Danish House, Arts and Crafts
PO Box 502, Maidstone, Kent ME17 3UZ
Needlework supplies including hardanger fabrics and tapes

Dryad
PO Box 38, Northgates, Leicester LE1 9BU
Craft and needlework supplies including rug yarn

Jane's Pincushion
Wroxham Barns, Tunstead Road, Hoveton,
Norwich NR12 8QU
Embroidery, tapestry and lacemaking supplies

Just Sew Fabrics and Crafts
Rotherfield Road, Jarvis Brook, Crowborough, East Sussex
Handicraft supplies including needlework

Kineton Gallery
Banbury Street, Kineton, Warwickshire CV35 0JS
Embroidery and lacemaking supplies, canvas and embroidery fabrics

Richmond Art and Craft
181 City Road, Cardiff CF2 3JB
All needlework supplies

Royal School of Needlework
25 Prince's Gate, London SW7 1QE
Needlework supplies including Paterna Persian Yarn

Spring blossoms

Materials and techniques

Fabric: cream or beige medium-weight linen or linen-type fabric

Threads: Anchor Stranded Cotton, one skein of each of the colours shown.

Techniques: satin stitch, long-and-short stitch, stem stitch, lazy daisy stitch

You can embroider this colourful Easter bouquet on other fabrics too. Trace off the outlines of the embroidery illustrated below and transfer it to the fabric following the instructions on page 13 or draw it freehand if you are good at drawing.

Anchor Stranded Cotton

	1		25		278
	293		28		924
	297		95		268
	316		98		363

Fabric: white, cream or beige medium-weight linen or 'linen-look' synthetic fabric
Threads: Anchor Stranded Cotton, 4 strands; Anchor Pearl Cotton No. 5
Techniques: satin stitch, French knots

Delicate colours call for delicate fabrics, and this pretty design should be kept as dainty as possible. You can, of course, set the design out differently on the cloth – the table and cloth size are an important factor in deciding how the motifs are positioned – or you could use the design for napkins or place mats instead.

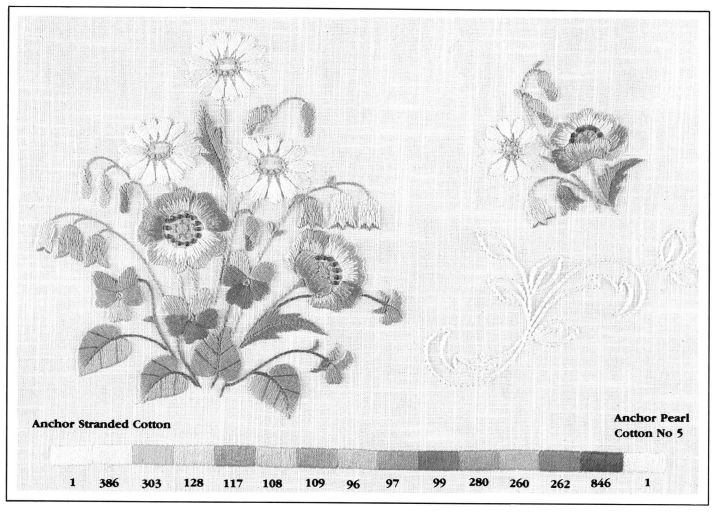

Anchor Stranded Cotton

Anchor Pearl Cotton No 5

| 1 | 386 | 303 | 128 | 117 | 108 | 109 | 96 | 97 | 99 | 280 | 260 | 262 | 846 | 1 |

Early crocuses

This pattern is embroidered on cream-coloured hardanger fabric and worked from a chart like those used for canvas-work patterns. The stitch is cross-stitch, but you can use different stitches as well if you like. Each square on the chart represents one stitch and the stitches are all worked over two threads of the fabric using the strands of Anchor Stranded Cotton. You can make the design smaller by working over just one thread or larger by working over three or more, but remember to use more or fewer strands of thread accordingly.

18

Anchor Stranded Cotton   I *light yellow* V *yellow* ◣ *deep yellow* ❙ *orange* ╱ *light mauve* ○ *mauve* N *deep mauve*

● *dark mauve* ┝ *light green* ✕ *green* ◢ *dark green* ╋ *blue green* ━ ━ ◺ *grey* ╱ *olive green* · *white*

The proud cockerel

Materials and techniques

Fabric: even-weave linen, beige
Threads: Anchor Stranded Cotton, 2, 3, or 4 strands according to size of motif
Techniques: cross-stitch

Make a tracing of the embroidered motif and transfer it to the fabric, enlarging or reducing if required. Our motif was embroidered following a pre-drawn design and is approximately 12·5in (32cm), with each stitch going across four threads.

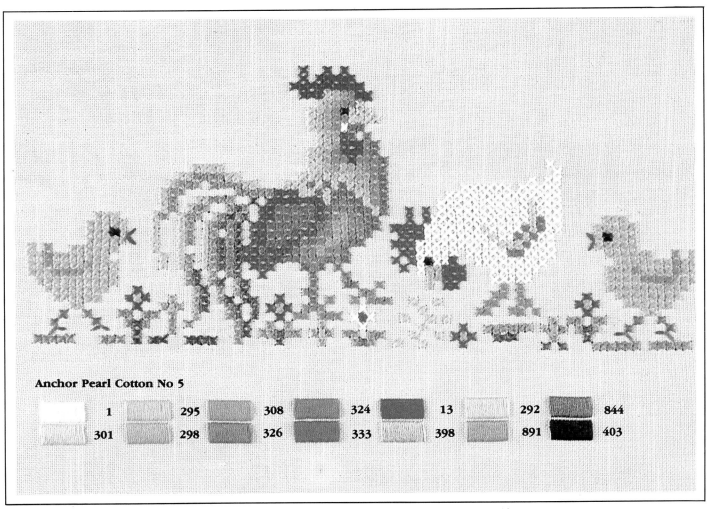

Anchor Pearl Cotton No 5

1	295	308	324	13	292	844
301	298	326	333	398	891	403

Happy Easter

Materials and techniques
Fabric: medium-weight textured even-weave fabric, brown, 56×64in (140×160cm)
Threads: Anchor Stranded Cotton, 3 to 4 strands; Anchor Pearl Cotton
Techniques: Darning stitch (see below), stem stitch, French knot, satin stitch, lazy daisy stitch

An Easter tablecloth to delight your children – Mother Goose takes her newly hatched chick for his first Easter promenade. The stitches are all explained and illustrated on pages 10 and 11, with the exception of the darning stitch. This is used for Mother Goose's shawl, and is simply straight diagonal stitches loosely interwoven with straight stitches going in the other direction.

Anchor

Stranded Cotton   **Anchor Pearl Cotton No 5**

1	300	314	97	111	160	162	280	267	403	1	397	49	334	302

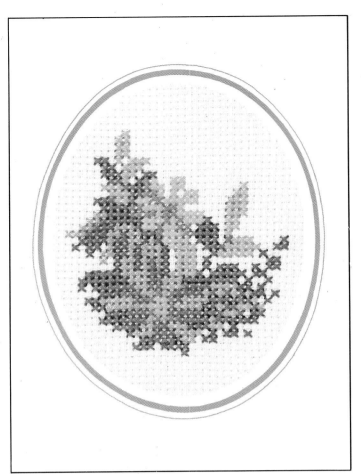 

Easter greeting cards

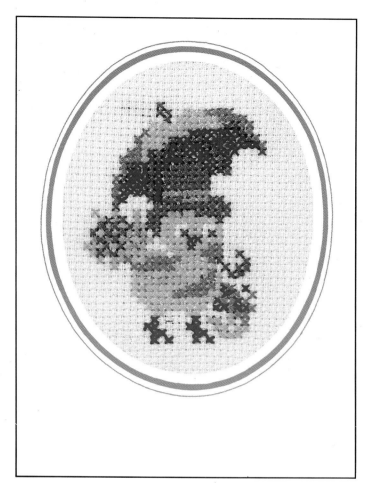

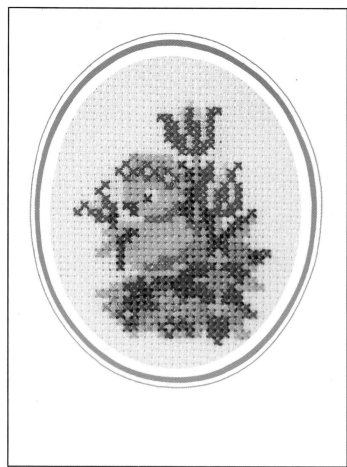

Materials

Fabric: woven (Aida) cotton or other coarse even-weave fabric
Threads: Anchor Stranded Cotton or Anchor Soft Embroidery
Small envelope
One sheet of white cardboard (mounting board is ideal)
No. 20 tapestry needle

With a little patience you can make this card in a couple of hours. The embroidery is cross-stitch, so you don't need to transfer the designs. Just work from the illustrations, counting the number of stitches. We recommend embroidering the crosses over two fabric threads, but you will need to count out the fabric squares beforehand to make sure your motif does not turn out too large. In order to give the embroideries the right background we mounted them on the front of a folded sheet of cardboard with an oval cut-out and added a decorative golden edging, but if you find the oval cut-out too difficult, an oblong one would be equally effective. You can write your own personal message on the inside of the card.

Easter eggs and cosies

These embroidered Easter eggs and cosies are worked in cross-stitch on either white or yellow hardanger fabric, using the charts opposite. The pattern for the egg cosies is below, so use this as a cutting guide, remembering to add the seam allowance, indicated by the dotted line. The pattern for the egg cosies is opposite.

Use Anchor Stranded Cotton for the embroidery, choosing your own colours, and make the stitches over one or two fabric threads depending on how big you want the motifs to be. The completed eggs should be filled with a little cotton wool to give them a good shape, and the cosies can be lined with fluffy quilting fabric for additional padding. That way your eggs will stay warm longer at breakfast time.

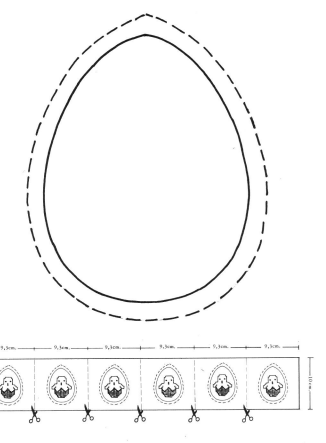

The motifs shown on this page can be used for either Easter eggs or cosies.

Before you start embroidering check the number of crosses to make sure that the pattern fits on to the fabric you are using.

⊡ *yellow* ✒ *blue*   ◣ *mauve* ~~~ ◥ *red*   •••• ◣ *green*   --- ‖ *gold*   ∞∞ ● *dark grey*   · *white*

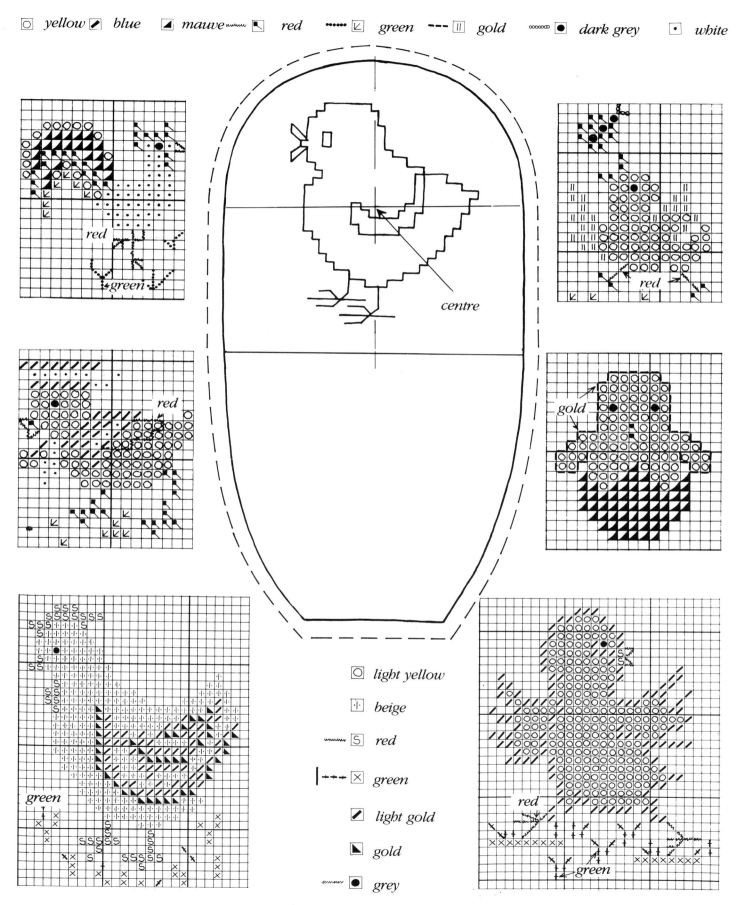

centre

⊡ *light yellow*

·⫶· *beige*

~~~ Ⓢ *red*

|--→ ☒ *green*

✒ *light gold*

◥ *gold*

~~~ ● *grey*

25

A motif for all seasons

A graceful, curving but simple design you can draw yourself

Materials and techniques

Fabric: medium-weight linen or synthetic linen-type fabric
Threads: Anchor Stranded Cotton, 3 or 4 strands, or Anchor Pearl Cotton No. 5
Techniques: stem stitch, satin stitch

You can use this pattern for a host of different purposes – tablecloth, cushions, oven glove, teacosy or curtains. On the following pages we give the pattern repeats for the square tablecloth but you can adapt this in many ways, making it bigger or smaller following the instructions on page 13.

There are no limits to the variations on this design – you can work it in outline stitches as shown, or you can fill in areas with satin and long-and-short stitch for a more traditional look. The colours you choose will make it look quite different, too, and you can arrange the motifs in an almost endless variety of ways.

Edge motif

The central motif

With the aid of a piece of tracing paper and a pencil you can easily draw the outlines of the motif, and can then enlarge or reduce it following the instructions on page 13 before transferring it on to your working fabric.

However, before you transfer the pattern on to the fabric we do recommend that you mark the centre of this drawing and the edge of the cloth with small dots, which will enable you to position the design correctly on the cloth. First transfer the quarter motif you have copied from our pattern on to the fabric. Fold the sheet over so that the marker points lie on top of one another and repeat this process until all four quarters of the central motif have been transferred.

Repeat this process with the motifs for the edges.

Edges and cushion

This drawing is suitable for both items (note the marker points). The cushion should be 15¾ in (40 cm) square, the drawing is 12½ in (32 cm) in size, which leaves you 1½ in (4 cm) of fabric on each side for turning a hem. If you draw the four pattern repeats using this pattern and place one on each corner of the fabric, you can easily see whether you like the design arranged like this.

centre of cushion

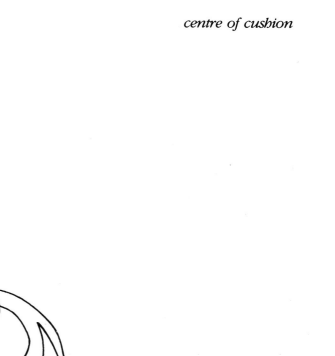

Embroidered hand towels

The type of hand-towels made with inwoven cotton strips are ideal for embroidering with a fairly fine thread such as Anchor Pearl Cotton No. 8. You will find some embroidery ideas on the opposite page. The colours listed are only meant to give you ideas and can be adapted according to the colour of the towel you finally select.

You will find the alphabet particularly useful, as towels embroidered with names or initials make extremely glamorous and unusual gifts. They would make a splendid Mother's Day present.

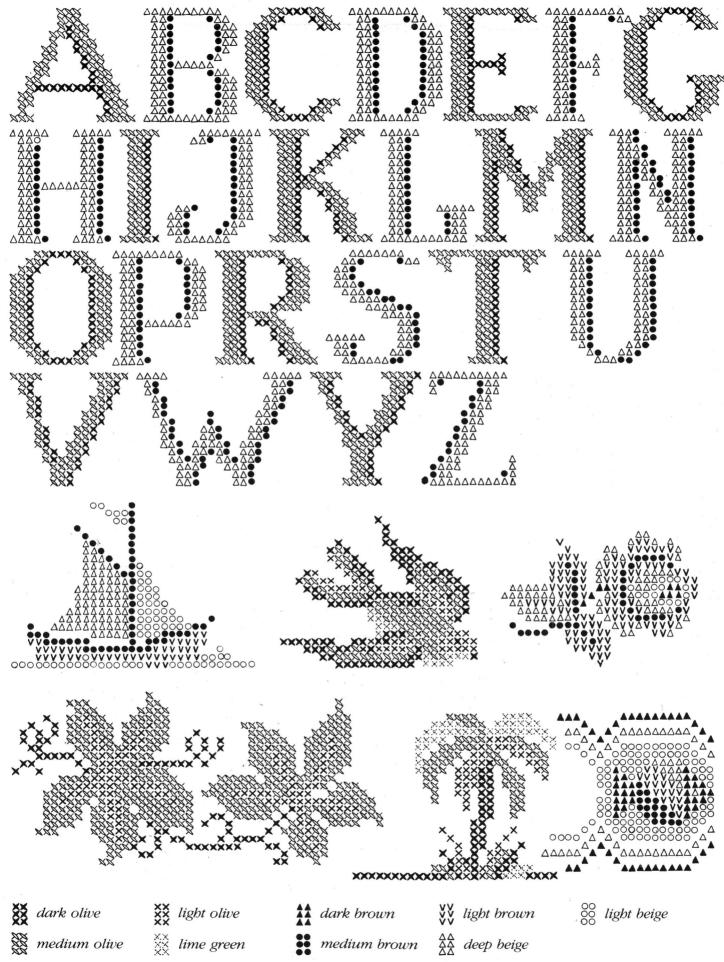

✖ *dark olive*	✖ *light olive*	▲ *dark brown*	⌄ *light brown*	○ *light beige*
✖ *medium olive*	⋮ *lime green*	● *medium brown*	△ *deep beige*	

Meadow flower kitchen set

You can give your kitchen an added sparkle with this decorative counted-thread work. The ready-made hand-towels and aprons made in a special even-weave fabric suitable for embroidery can sometimes be bought from specialist suppliers, and the charts assume that this type of fabric is being used. However, the embroidery pattern can easily be adapted to free style by the transferring of outline method explained on page 13. Use Anchor Stranded Cotton, suiting the number of strands to the thickness of the fabric. You should be able to use up all your cotton remnants for this embroidery because the flower motifs can be worked in whatever colours you choose – those given on the pattern are only suggestions.

on brown-striped towels and aprons

on yellow-striped towels and aprons

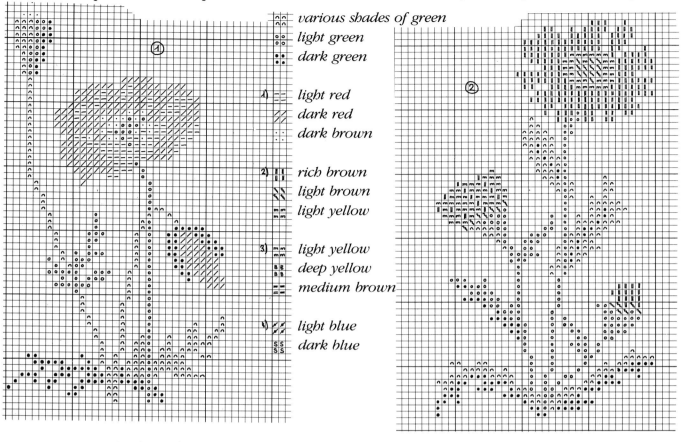

① ②

	various shades of green
	light green
	dark green
1)	light red
	dark red
	dark brown
2)	rich brown
	light brown
	light yellow
3)	light yellow
	deep yellow
	medium brown
4)	light blue
	dark blue

on green-striped towels and aprons

on rust-red striped towels

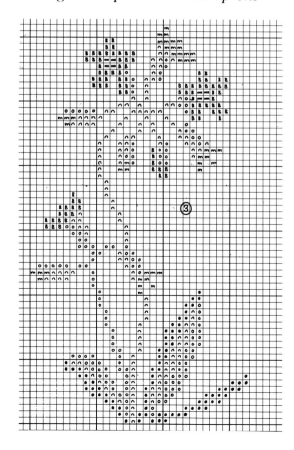 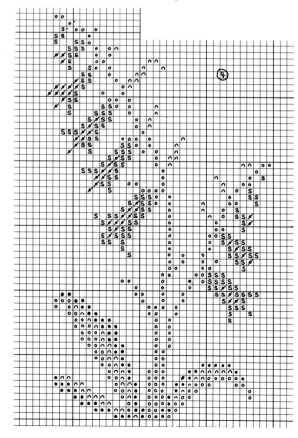

③ ④

Roses which never fade

Materials and techniques

Fabric: Fine linen or linen-type fabric, white.
Threads: Anchor Stranded Cotton, 4 strands; Anchor Pearl Cotton No. 5
Techniques: satin stitch, stem stitch, French knots

This dream of a cloth will enhance any table, but it's only for very special occasions. You can transfer the pattern by tracing off the outline given on the next page and following the instructions on page 13. If you haven't the time to embroider a whole tablecloth, try the little sprigs of violets as a motif for napkins or handkerchiefs.

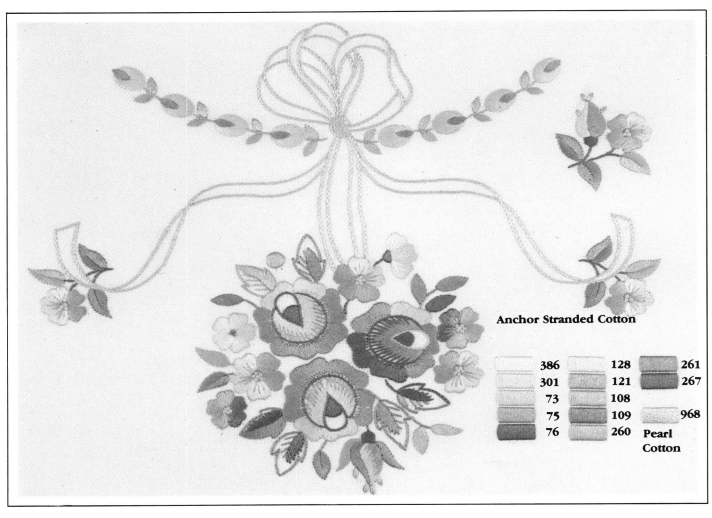

Anchor Stranded Cotton

386	128	261
301	121	267
73	108	
75	109	968
76	260	**Pearl Cotton**

34

Make a tracing of this design and then enlarge or reduce it using the technique explained on page 13. You can arrange the 'floral bouquets' on the fabric as we have done them or in whatever way appeals to you.

Everlasting cactus plants

These little cactus pictures are embroidered in
cross-stitch over two threads of a fairly loosely
woven linen fabric. Use Anchor Soft Embroidery
or Anchor Stranded Cotton and select several
shades of green, adding a touch of colour with a
few reds or yellows. Pictures such as these make
delightful gifts, particularly when simply framed
in natural wood like those illustrated.

Summer flowers in cross-stitch

Materials

Fabric: medium-weight even-weave linen, white. We recommend buying a plain tablecloth with the edges already finished.

Threads: Anchor Stranded Cotton, 3 or 4 strands, Coton à Broder or Pearl Cotton No. 5

The size of the table you are making the cloth for will determine the layout of the motifs, but the way they are placed in squares means that they can be repeated as often as needed to fill the space. Before you start working mark the exact centre on your fabric, also marking the size of the table so that the motifs don't go over the edges. First embroider the lines of cross-stitch, outlining each square. Embroidering the flower motifs, following the chart, is then very easy.

The design should be embroidered over two or three fabric threads, making a cross of about ⅛ in (4 mm).

Anchor Stranded Cotton							
○ 95	✕ 35	● 99	◣ 842	▲ 307	∪ 370	◨ 257	⊤ 262
⋈ 40	∅ 97	△ 843	△ 305	✕ 310	∨ 265	＋ 266

Wild strawberries

Materials and techniques

Fabric: fine or medium-weight linen suitable for a tablecloth. Or buy a ready-made tablecloth.

Threads: Anchor Stranded Cotton, 3 or 4 strands, depending on weight of fabric

Techniques: satin stitch, long-and-short stitch, stem stitch, French knots

These strawberries, unlike the edible variety, remain fresh for ever. Transfer our design from the colour ilustration, using the method described on page 13. The motif could be used to advantage to make a charming set of place mats or napkins, and it would not need enlarging or reducing.

Anchor Stranded Cotton

| 975 | 295 | 260 | 255 | 257 | 11 | 13 | 969 |

Everlasting flowers

Materials and techniques

Fabric: fine or medium-weight linen suitable for a tablecloth. Or buy a ready-made tablecloth. We have used one with a pretty woven edging.

Threads: Anchor Stranded Cotton, 3 or 4 strands, depending on the thickness of the fabric. The lazy daisy stitch can be done with the full thickness of thread.

Techniques: satin stitch, stem stitch, French knots and lazy daisy stitch Trace off the design from the colour illustration, bearing in mind that you may have to enlarge it slightly to fit the cloth (see page 13 for technique). Our motif is approximately 23½ in (60 cm) square, but obviously the deciding factor is the size of the table you will be using.

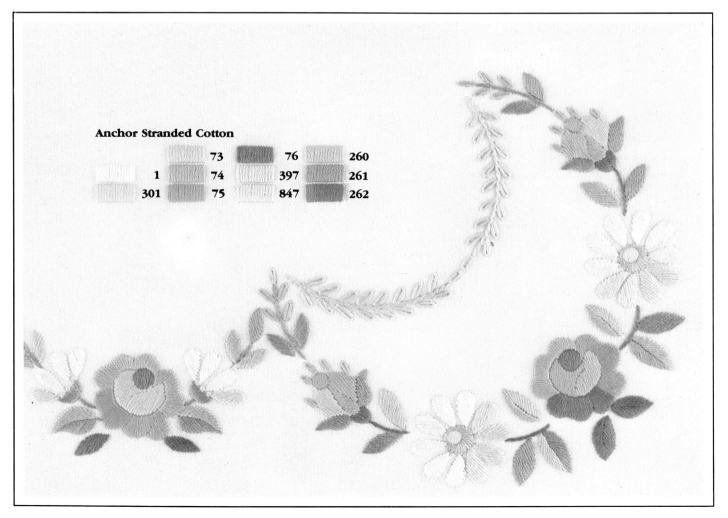

Anchor Stranded Cotton

73	76	260
1	74	397	261
301	75	847	262

Country holiday teacloths

These linen cloths have special woven panels intended to make cross-stitch embroidery simpler, but if you cannot obtain similar items use the charming designs for another purpose. You could embroider a picture like that shown on the next page, or you could make embroidered greetings cards such as those on pages 22-23.

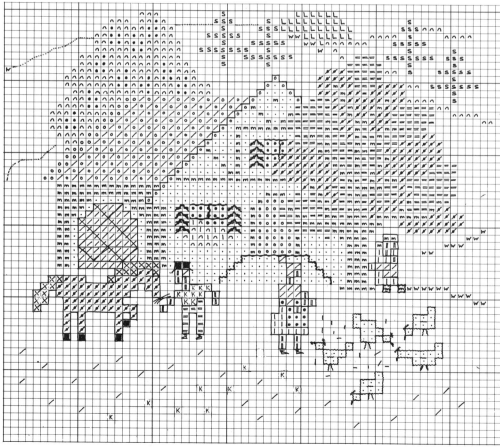

		dark green
		light green
		dark blue
		light blue
B B		dark brown
• •		medium brown
X X		light brown
K K		yellow
∧ ∧		red
◥◣		pink
o o		ochre
m m		rust
∕∕		salmon
∙∙		flesh colour

Backstitch

	black
	medium brown
	dark green
	rust
⁄	blue
	red
‖‖	yellow

X X	beige
∕∕	light brown
s s	medium brown
m m	dark brown
⋈ ⋈	green-brown
o o	red-brown
∕∕	rust brown
= =	orange-brown
∧ ∧	green
• ∙	pale yellow
L L	yellow
∙ ∙	white
I I	red
‖ ‖	flesh colour
K K	grey
■ ■	black

Backstitch

	black
	dark brown
	orange-brown
	green-brown

Going to the mountains

Materials

Fabric: a piece of cream linen fabric about 15¾×19¾ in (40×50 cm) with 8 threads to ⅜ in (1 cm)

Threads: Anchor Stranded Cotton

Those who have been on holiday in Austria or Switzerland may have seen the farmers driving the cows up into the Alpine mountain pastures where they will spend the summer in peace and solitude, the bells round their necks ringing as they move from place to place.

This charming wall picture will enhance any home, whether it has personal associations or not, and is quite quick to make as it's all done in cross-stitch worked over two fabric threads. Transfer the design from our colour picture using the technique described on page 13, and either use our picture as a guide for the colours or vary them acccording to your own ideas. When the picture is finished you can hem it along the cross-stitched border, sew loops along the upper edge and insert a rod to hang it up by.

Build a house

Materials

Fabric: 1 piece of cream linen fabric about 12×20 in (30×50 cm) with 20 threads to 1 in (2·5 cm)
Threads: Anchor Stranded Cotton

Wooden frame: a length of about 2¾ yards (2½ metres) of wood baton ⅜ in × 1 in (1 cm × 3 cm); piece of hardboard or plywood measuring 9½ × 14½ in (24 × 37 cm) for back wall: wood glue

With a little patience you can build this farmhouse, complete with its stables and storehouse. Only the walls and roof are made of wood. The contents and the inhabitants are all embroidered, using cross-stitch over two threads of fabric.

It is wisest to do the embroidery first (trace it off from the picture on the following page) and then start on the wooden construction; otherwise you might find that the contents did not fit the house. If you don't feel you can cope with the carpentry ask your husband or boyfriend to help, but it is quite a simple construction. The best way to do it is to cut the hardboard or plywood to size and then trim the embroidery so that it is just about ¼ in (5 mm) smaller than the hardboard all the way round. Cut the wood batons to the

44

measurements given below, assemble and glue them and leave them to dry. When they are dry, run glue carefully round the edge of the hardboard, place the tapestry in position on it and put the entire wooden assembly on top, weighting it while the glue dries.

Harvest festival

Rye, oats, wheat and barley are the motifs for these
delightful cross-stitch pictures

Materials

Fabric: a piece of cream-coloured linen about
10×20 cm (25×50 cm) with 11 threads to ⅜ in
(1 cm)
Threads: Anchor Stranded Cotton, 3 strands; 2
strands for the outline

These pictures, 7×17 in (18×43 cm) in size, are
worked in cross-stitch over two fabric threads,
except for the outlines, which are done in
backstitch using only 2 strands of thread.

The patterns and suggested colour-schemes are
on page 48.

Corn and flowers

A tablecloth with a feeling of late-summer ripeness

Materials and techniques

Fabric: brown 'linen-look' fabric or slightly textured cotton. Or buy a ready-made brown tablecloth.

Threads: Anchor Stranded Cotton, 4 strands

Techniques: satin stitch, French knots, lazy daisy stitch (the sides of the ears of corn)

This lovely autumnal tablecloth will create a Harvest Festival atmosphere in your home.

The complete motif is given on page 49, so trace this off and enlarge or reduce it if necessary. The motifs can be placed in any manner you choose, or you can follow the way we have arranged them. We have used just three colours – a pale cream, a pale gold and a darker gold – but you can choose your own according to the colour of the fabric.

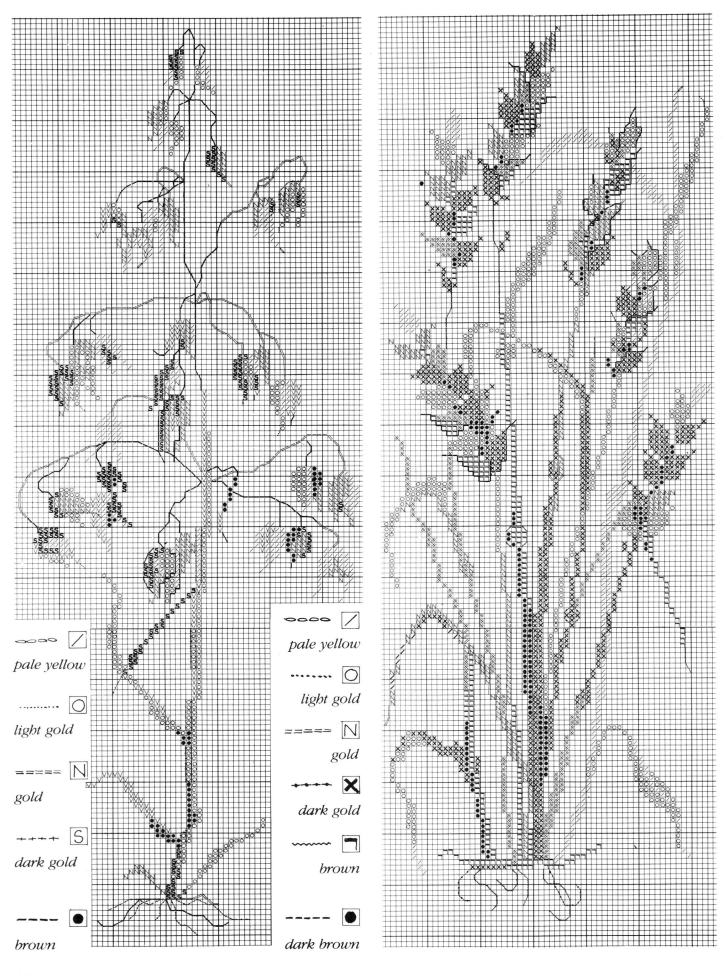

∘∘∘∘ ／
pale yellow

·········· ○
light gold

===== N
gold

++++ S
dark gold

● ● ● ●
brown

∘∘∘∘ ／
pale yellow

·········· ○
light gold

===== N
gold

✕
dark gold

∼∼∼∼ ⌐
brown

----- ●
dark brown

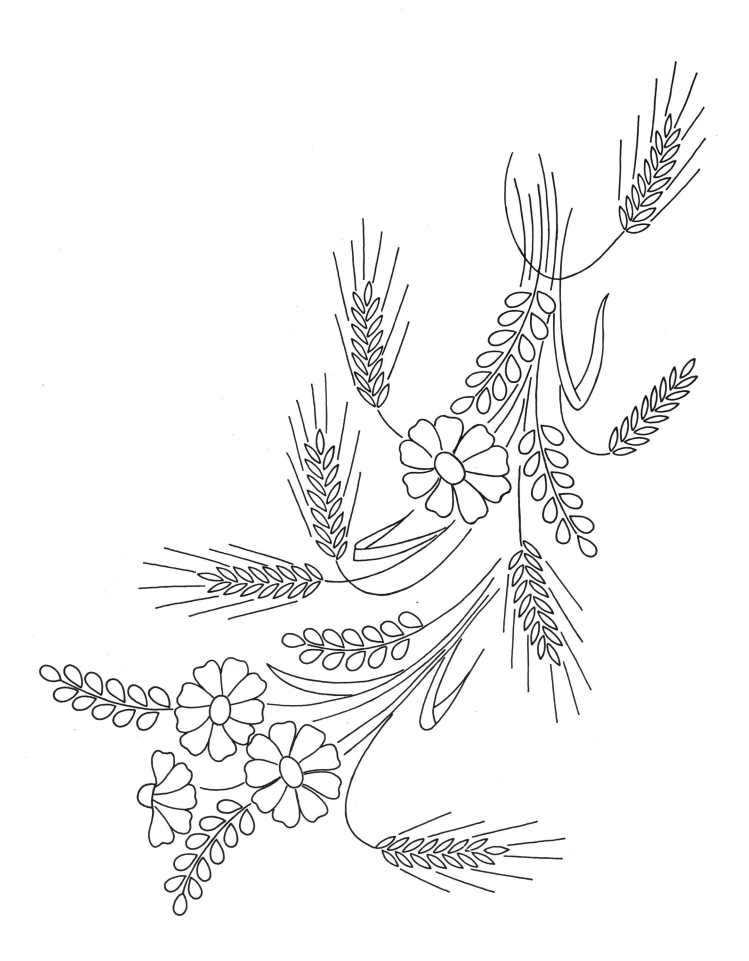

Toadstools

Materials

Fabric: cream-coloured even-weave linen

Embroidery threads: Anchor Stranded Cotton or Soft Embroidery

It may not be edible, but this red toadstool with white spots is delightful to look at and makes a nice design. This autumn tablecloth can be worked on linen or cotton using cross-stitch over two or three fabric threads. If you like, you can embroider the outlines using straight stitches and 3 strands of thread. The chart gives you the colour numbers and each individual colour has been allocated its own symbol. You will need approximately one hank of thread per colour. Don't forget to mark the centre of the design on the tablecloth before you start working.

Anchor Stranded Cotton

□ 301
⊠ 11
✕ 13
◹ 369
◤ 370
○ 374
● 372
△ 260
∨ 261
▲ 262
■ 882
✕ 933

Wayside flowers

Materials and techniques

Fabric: cream-coloured linen, linen-type fabric or cotton suitable for a tablecloth. Or buy a ready-made tablecloth.
Threads: Anchor Stranded Cotton, 4 strands
Techniques: Satin stitch, stem stitch, lazy daisy stitch

The colours used for this design are gentle autumnal ones, ranging from dark green to light olive, plus white and the softest of yellows. These delicate ferns and grasses need a light touch, so this is not an embroidery for beginners. It's a useful design, though, as any of the motifs could be used singly for a small item, and you can adapt the pattern section shown below to give yourself further ideas for the layout on the tablecloth.

Pots and pans

Shiny polished copper pots make nice wall decorations, and so do pictures of them

Fabric: medium-weight even-weave linen, white

Embroidery threads: Anchor Stranded Cotton, 2 strands

These little pictures are about 3½×4¼ in (9×11 cm) in size and are embroidered on even-weave linen in cross-stitch. Simply framed, they are an attractive decoration for the living room or kitchen, and they make a good beginner's project for anyone unused to working from embroidery charts. We have chosen two of these for you to work from – see if you can draw up your own charts for the others.

I *yellow*   U *light gold*   ⅂ *gold*   ---- ★ *dark gold*

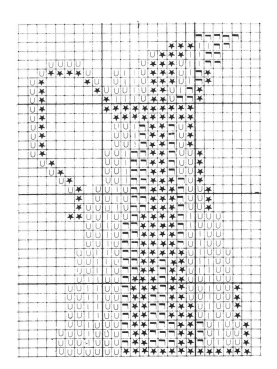
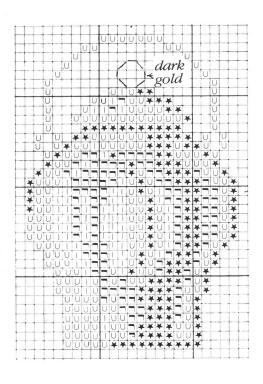

dark gold

Kitchen tray-holder

This is a practical and useful idea – an ideal gift. You can make such an article for your kitchen or for someone else's with very little effort.

All you need is 2 yards (2 metres) of hardanger tape, which does not need to be hemmed because it has two woven edges, a wooden ring and some Anchor Stranded Cotton. Work the motifs from our simple charts, and you will be amazed at how quickly you can complete the job. Use two strands of thread throughout. Hardanger fabric and tape are available from the Danish House (see page 15).

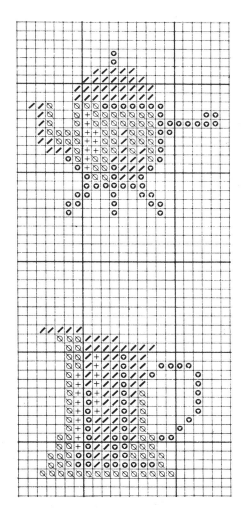

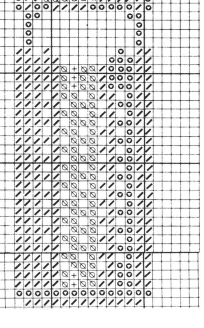

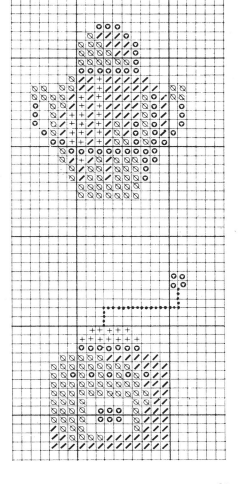

∞	+	yellow
⋀⋀⋀⋀⋀	⌀	light brown
	╱	brown
••••	◬	dark brown

Cross-stitch clock

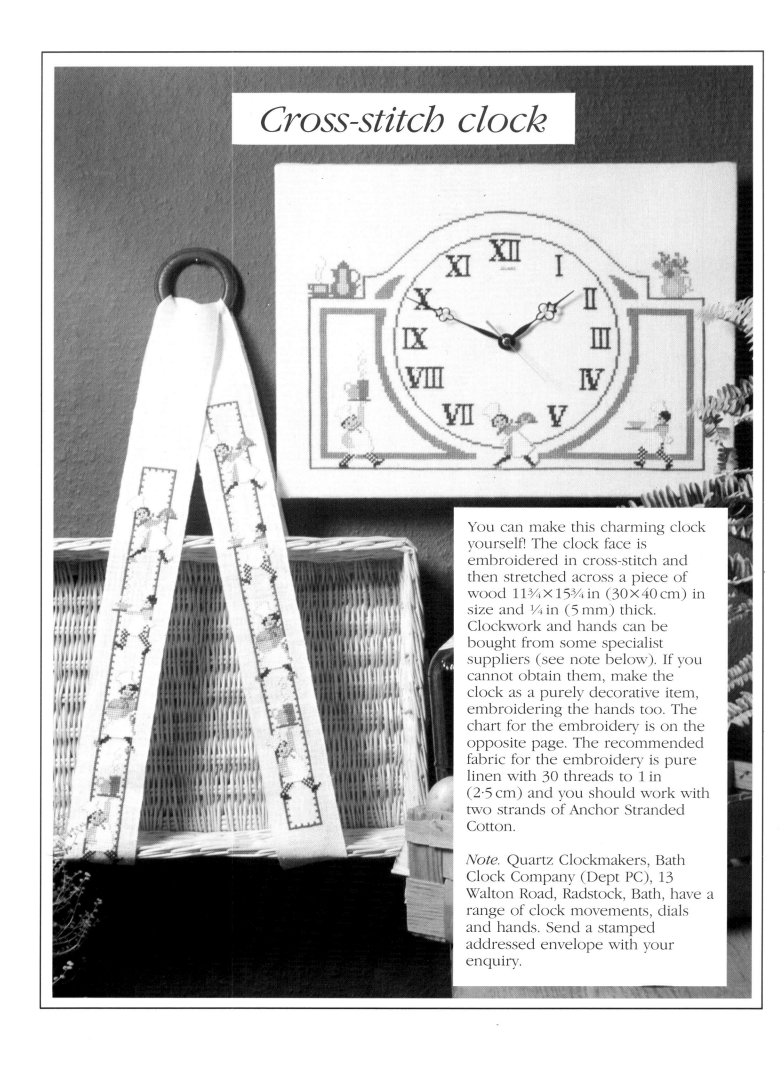

You can make this charming clock yourself! The clock face is embroidered in cross-stitch and then stretched across a piece of wood 11¾×15¾ in (30×40 cm) in size and ¼ in (5 mm) thick. Clockwork and hands can be bought from some specialist suppliers (see note below). If you cannot obtain them, make the clock as a purely decorative item, embroidering the hands too. The chart for the embroidery is on the opposite page. The recommended fabric for the embroidery is pure linen with 30 threads to 1 in (2·5 cm) and you should work with two strands of Anchor Stranded Cotton.

Note. Quartz Clockmakers, Bath Clock Company (Dept PC), 13 Walton Road, Radstock, Bath, have a range of clock movements, dials and hands. Send a stamped addressed envelope with your enquiry.

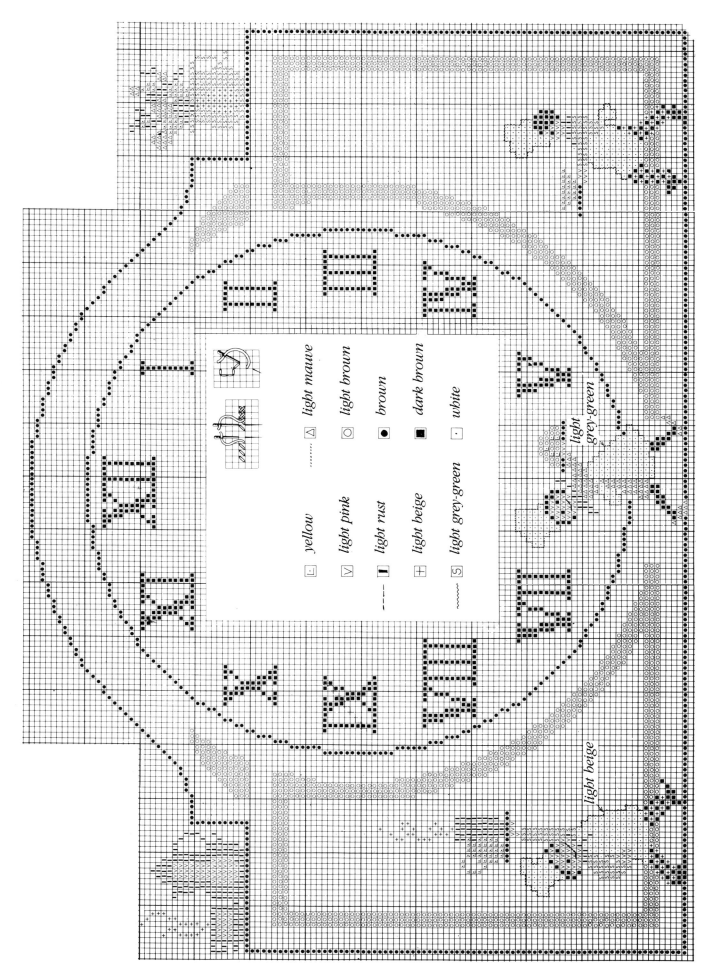

light
grey-green

light beige

	yellow		light mauve
	light pink	○	light brown
▬	light rust	●	brown
+	light beige	■	dark brown
S	light grey-green	·	white

Traditional sampler

This cross-stitch sampler was based on an antique one of the type done in our grandmothers' young days. These used to record the details of the person's life, using words and pictures, and were also a way of demonstrating a young person's skill in embroidery.

You can use the alphabet and numbers on the opposite page to embroider personal data such as birth date, wedding date and so on. Our sampler is done on coarse, even-weave linen using Anchor Soft Embroidery, but you can use Anchor Stranded Cotton if you prefer and embroider over two or three fabric threads according to what size you want to make it.

You could use up thread remnants with this project since you can choose whatever colours you like. When the sampler is finished stretch the fabric over a board, turning the edges over the back and mitring the corners. This board can then be glued on to a larger, plain-coloured base, as in the photograph. This is an easy and effective way of mounting an embroidery.

light olive

dark brown

dark olive

light rust-red

dark rust red

orange

dark red

white

light red

stem stitch in
light brown

medium brown

satin stitch in
light brown

light beige

deep beige

light rust-red

dark brown

light mauve

French knots in
deep mauve

Autumn pot pourri

Materials and techniques

Fabric: Cream medium-weight linen or cotton
Threads: Anchor Stranded Cotton, 3 or 4 strands
Techniques: satin stitch, stem stitch, French knots, lazy daisy stitch

In autumn wild-flower enthusiasts go to great lengths to seek out grasses, leaves and flowers which they then dry and arrange in vases. This looks very nice, but what better way of capturing the feel of autumn for ever than making one of our autumn cushions or the lovely tablecloth?

Trace off the pattern opposite and, for the cushion, enlarge it (see page 13) to about 10 in (25 cm) square. The amount you enlarge the tablecloth motif will, of course, depend on the size of the cloth. The cushion should be cut to measure about 15¾ in (40 cm) square.

EMBROIDERING FOR CHRISTMAS

The days are getting shorter, the weather is becoming colder and the preparations are beginning for the year's most important celebration. So why not make sure you have an appropriate tablecloth? On these pages you can see two embroidery designs which are ideally suited for the pre-Christmas period, as they are both quite easy to do. And if you haven't finished for this Christmas, there will be another one next year. Both cloths are embroidered on medium-weight linen, and you can use Anchor Stranded Cotton (four strands) or Anchor Pearl Cotton

No. 5. The stitches are stem stitch and satin stitch.

For both these cloths the motifs can be arranged according to your own requirements and the size of the table. If you are a confident designer and seamstress, you could make tablecloths in other shapes, such as a six-pointed star, a round cover or a rectangular table-centre. An embroidered tablecloth looks very attractive with a fancy hem or a lace or crochet border, such as those you can buy in department stores.

Christmas tree ornaments

These mini-embroideries, suitable for beginners with little experience, are ideal for children, who always like having a hand in making the decorations. All the items are in cross-stitch, and are quick and easy to embroider.

Such items can be used as decorations for the Christmas tree, present tags or even for putting little gifts in.

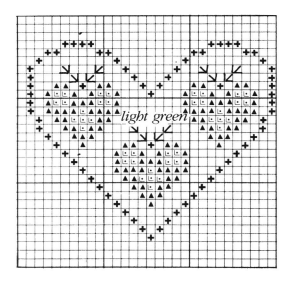

light green

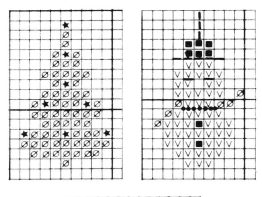

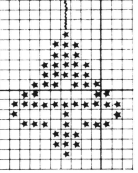

Father Christmas will soon be here

These designs are embroidered in cross-stitch on coloured woven cotton (Aida) fabric and hessian. Both are particularly suitable for patterns where the squares are counted out. They are worked in Anchor Soft Embroidery thread, but you could add a little extra sparkle by using gold or silver threads as well.

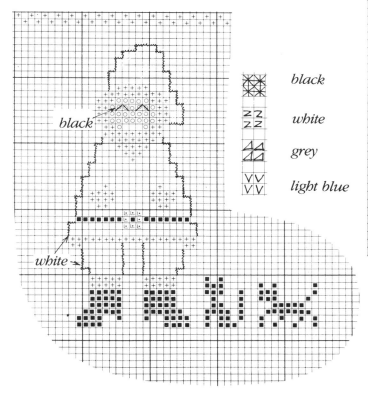

✳	black
z	white
△	grey
V	light blue

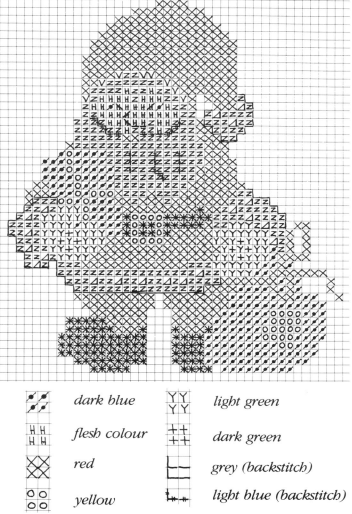

dark blue		Y	light green
H	flesh colour	+	dark green
✕	red		grey (backstitch)
O	yellow		light blue (backstitch)

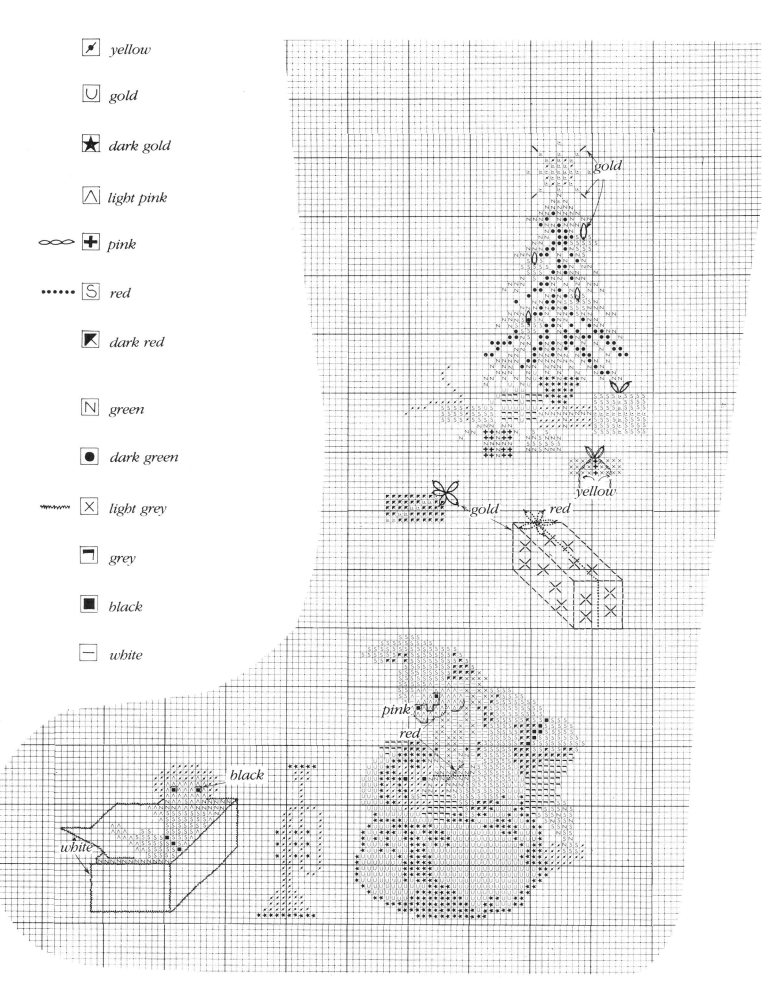

yellow

gold

dark gold

light pink

pink

red

dark red

green

dark green

light grey

grey

black

white

gold

yellow

gold   red

pink

red

black

white

Christmas stockings

Materials

Fabric: woven cotton (Aida) fabric, embroidery canvas or heavy linen with 16 threads to 1 in (2½ cm)

Threads: Anchor Soft Embroidery or Anchor Stranded Cotton

Any child who hangs up one of these embroidered stockings on the evening of December 24th is bound to find lots of surprises next morning. To avoid any family mix-ups if there are two or more children, the design should be embroidered on fabric of different colours. You could easily embroider the name of the child, too, if you have the time. The stitch is cross-stitch and the combined embroidery chart and cutting-out pattern are on the opposite page.

Cut out two pieces for each stocking and sew them together with bias binding for a neat, ornamental finish.

The Advent calendar

Advent calendars are mainly a Continental custom, but they are beginning to catch on in Britain and America, and children, not surprisingly, love them, as they begin the excitement of Christmas 24 days in advance. As you can see from the picture our calendar designs can also be used for a tablecloth, and they are all worked in quick cross-stitch.

The designs should be embroidered on a coarse fabric such as jute or hessian or a coarse woollen fabric. Work in cross-stitch, using backstitch or stem stitch for the outlines. We would recommend Anchor Stranded Cotton, Soft Embroidery or Tapisserie Wool.

The brass rings are available from craft shops or the soft furnishings departments of stores and can be attached with a few stitches under each embroidered number.

New sparkle for your kitchen

These three embroidery motifs will give your kitchen that personal feeling so many kitchens lack. Towels, apron, tablecloths – there are lots of things you can use these motifs on in the kitchen. Since this type of fabric is available in other colours, the designs can also be embroidered to match the appropriate decor.

We used tough hardanger kitchen fabric for the tablecloth, but you can also create a pretty effect by embroidering on check gingham or striped cotton. The towels and aprons were bought ready-made. The designs are worked in cross-stitch, and you can use Anchor Stranded Cotton, two or three strands, or Anchor Pearl Cotton. Follow our chart on the opposite page. The little round 'miniature' tapestries were embroidered on fine white tapestry canvas with 16 threads and put into the small round frames you can buy in craft shops.

Anchor Stranded Cotton

∂	light blue	128
v	medium blue	131
✗	dark blue	148

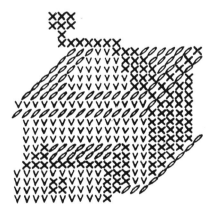

There's no doubt that these charmingly embroidered towels will enhance your kitchen.

The simple motifs suit the check cloth beautifully, but they could be used to equal effect on plain fabric or a different type of check.

Aprons embroidered in cross-stitch would make a delightful gift or sale item.

A child is born

A lovely embroidered wall plaque like these will always remind you of your child's birth. We have supplied a chart for the one at the top, which is worked in cross-stitch on even-weave linen using two strands of Anchor Stranded Cotton. The child's name and any important information about the birth, such as the precise time, and the baby's weight, can be put in. The plaque, when finished, can be fastened to a round piece of card and then hung up with a ribbon, or you could put it in an oval picture frame – either way it will look very charming.

⊡	very light pink/blue	▽	light pink	S	pink/blue	✕	deep pink	‖‖‖	very deep pink
C	very light red/blue	⊘	light red/blue	▼ - - - -	mauve	⊙	beige	○	very light brown
=	light brown	✕	brown	✗	red-brown	◕	dark brown	/	light green
Z	grey	⁄	green	6	light mauve	■ ∼∼∼	black	·	light grey

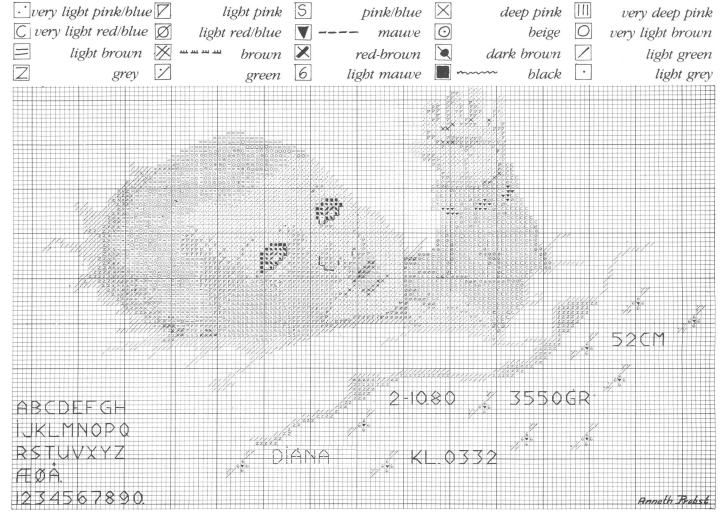

Jolly themes for the playroom

These motifs can be used in a number of ways – on a carpet, on cushion covers or as wall decorations as shown here. They are embroidered in cross-stitch or half-cross stitch on white canvas with approximately 8 threads to 1 in (2½ cm) using Paterna Persian yarn or a double thread of Anchor Tapisserie Wool. The area of each picture is 13¾ in (35 cm) square, and you will need to leave a border of at least 2 in (5 cm) all round. Try designing other simple motifs for yourself. Use a felt-tip pen and draw simple designs straight on to the canvas. You can then pick bright colours and fill in the areas with embroidery.

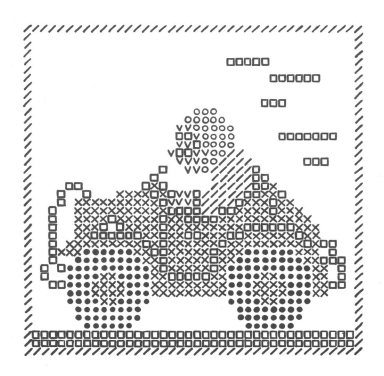

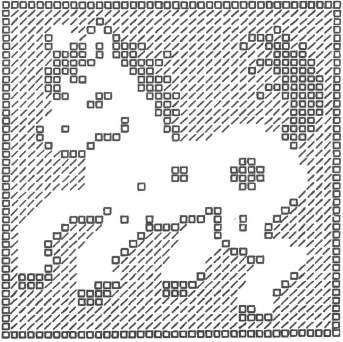

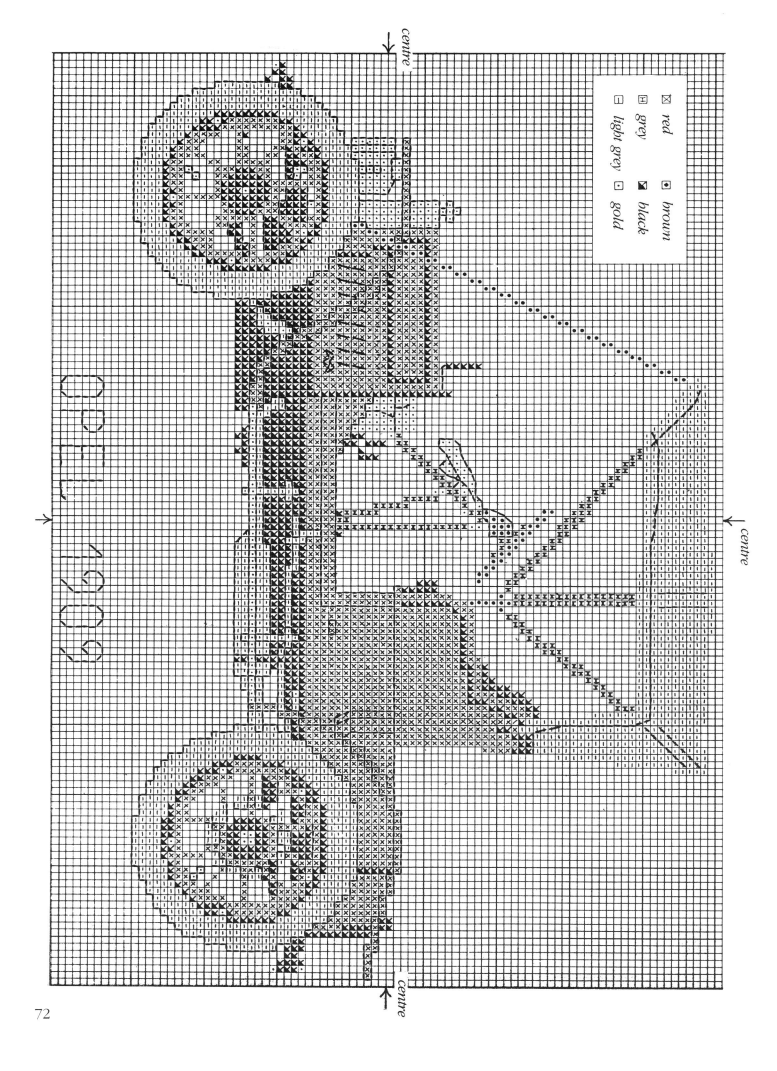

	red		brown
⊞	grey		black
⊟	light grey		gold

Vintage cars to embroider

These vintage cars, unlike the real thing, are within anybody's price range! We have given you a chart (opposite) for one, the 1909 Opel. It is worked on medium even-weave linen in cross-stitch over two fabric threads, using three strands of Anchor Stranded Cotton or Anchor Pearl Cotton No. 5. Use natural linen with not more than 30 threads to 1 in (2½ cm) and embroider following the chart. The picture should measure 11¾×15¾ in (30×40 cm), so buy enough to leave a border of at least 2 in (5 cm) all round. If you use touches of gold or silver thread you can create the effect of the chrome parts here and there.

Choose a mount of a toning colour and a natural-wood frame, which will further enhance your picture.

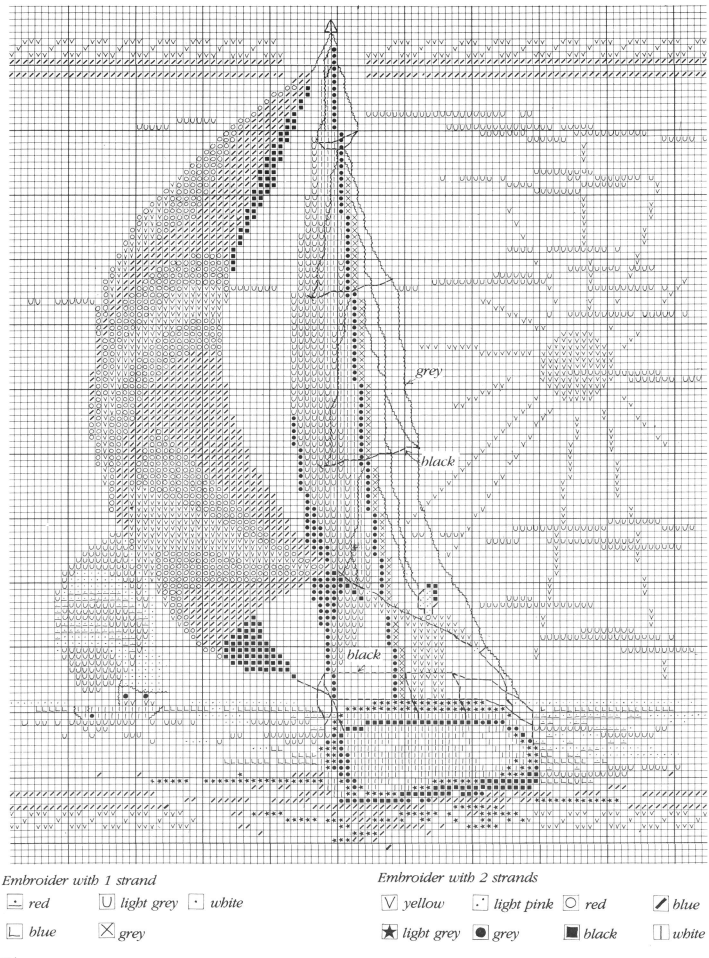

grey

black

black

Embroider with 1 strand

⊡ red   U light grey   · white

L blue   X grey

Embroider with 2 strands

V yellow   ∴ light pink   O red   ╱ blue

★ light grey   ● grey   ■ black   ‖ white

Leisure-time cushions

Cushions like these will put you in a holiday frame of mind even if you are just sitting in front of the fire at home. We have given you a chart (opposite) for the yacht design, which we believe will be the most popular, with its atmosphere of carefree days. It is worked in cross-stitch on coloured hardanger fabric, and the thread used is Anchor Stranded Cotton. The cushion is approximately 15¾ in (40 cm) square. When buying the fabric, remember that you must either purchase enough for the back of the cushion or else use a contrasting fabric for the back . This can look very nice, particularly if you finish the cushion by sewing a length of piping cord round the edges or embroider a decorative border.

Embroidered hours

This lovely Art Nouveau style clock has an embroidered border using brown and rust on beige-coloured fabric.

Materials

Fabric: beige embroidery linen or linen-type fabric
Backing: piece of hardboard 11¾×15¾ in (30×40 cm)
Glue: Uhu glue
Clock: clockwork and hands
Threads: Anchor Stranded Cotton in the following colours:

dark brown	No. 359
medium brown	No. 370
very dark rust	No. 341
dark rust	No. 340
medium rust	No. 338
light rust	No. 884
light beige	No. 368
medium beige	No. 369
deep beige	No. 370
black/brown	No. 382

The full-size embroidery pattern for the clock border is on the following pages, so trace this off and transfer it to your fabric. You can enlarge it if you need to accommodate larger clock hands, so buy the hands and clockwork before deciding (see **Note** below). Work the design in satin and stem stitch using three strands of thread only to give a fine finish. When the embroidery is complete, lay it face downwards and press it carefully using a damp cloth.

Now you must stretch it on to the hardboard, but first drill a hole in the middle of the hardboard approximately ⅜ in (1 cm) for the shaft for the clock hands.

Stretch the embroidery as follows. On the rough side of the hardboard glue a strip along the edge about ¾-1¼ in (2-3 cm) wide. Leave this for about ten minutes and, while it is drying, glue a strip the same width along the selvage of the fabric on the wrong side. As soon as the glue is tacky press the first side on, keeping the grain nice and straight, and then glue the opposite side in the same way, stretching the fabric across the hardboard with a light pressure and making sure the grain is kept straight. Repeat the process for the other two sides and then assemble the clock, pushing the hands arbor through the hole in the hardboard and then through the fabric (snip the fabric carefully to allow for this).

Fasten the clockwork according to the instructions, attach the clock hands – and your own embroidered clock is finished.

If you can find a suitable picture frame to give your clock that special touch, so much the better, but if you have stretched the fabric correctly it is not essential.

Note Quartz Clockmakers, Bath Clock Company (Dept PC), 13 Walton Road, Rudstock, Bath, have a range of clock movements, dials and hands. Send a stamped addressed envelope with your enquiry.

Index